101 U

for a

Yorkshire Pudding

written by
Ian McMillan
illustrated by
Tony Husband

Dalesman

First published in 2011 by Dalesman
an imprint of
Country Publications Ltd
The Water Mill, Broughton Hall
Skipton, North Yorkshire BD23 3AG
www.dalesman.co.uk

Text © Ian McMillan 2011
Cartoons © Tony Husband 2011

ISBN 978-1-85568-293-1

Typeset in Stone Informal.

Printed in China by 1010 Printing International Ltd.

Introduction

Welcome to this celebration of the White Rose County's greatest culinary export, the Yorkshire Pudding.

I regard myself as a bit of an expert in the making of Yorkshire Puddings, and the mixing of the batter is one of the highlights of my Sunday morning. I get my pinny on. I get the flour. I get the eggs. I get the milk. I get the pepper — because I love a peppery Yorkshire. I chuck the flour in the same bowl I've used for years. I never bother measuring because I always regard the making of the Yorkshires as fundamentally an improvisational performance, and that's why my Yorkshires are always a little bit different each week, and that's how it should be. I crack the eggs into the bowl. I add a bit of milk. I whisk with a fork until my arms ache, then I stop whisking for a moment, and then I whisk some more. Then I whisk some more, because you have to put the time in when you're making Yorkshires.

The lard is nice and hot. It's spitting at me. Time to put the Yorkshires in...

In the gap between putting the Yorkshires in the oven and getting them out, I often ponder on the different things you could use a Yorkshire Pudding for. And the idea for this book was born. And I got so excited about the idea that I burnt the puddings, and that's the first time that's ever happened!

Oh, and by the way: they're all made up...

Dear Sir,

Your article 'The History of the Yorkshire Pudding' in last week's issue reminded me of a story my granddad used to tell about his time in the First World War. His mate Sid Bedale from Bradford got a parcel from his wife containing a Yorkshire Pudding which she'd made for him "to keep him going through the war" as her note said.

Of course, the post being what it was in those days, by the time the pudding got to him on the Western Front it was rock-hard and inedible, but Sid put it in the pocket of his tunic as a keepsake to remind him of my grandma.

That morning my granddad and the rest of his mates had to go 'over the top' to attack the enemy lines a few hundred yards away; as a sergeant, Sid was first out of the trenches, leading his men into the field of battle. In a hail of German bullets, one caught him directly in the chest and he would have been killed but for my grandma's solid and steely Yorkshire pudding!

After the war he had it framed and hung up in their back kitchen!!

Yours, Ann Grimley

Variations on a theme of Yorkshire Puddings, part one

Yorkshire Cudding: What Yorkshire cows chew.

Yorkshire Budding: What Yorkshire plants do in spring.

Yorkshire Studding: A Tyke tackle in football. Yellow card!

Yorkshire Mudding: A beauty treatment. Mud from the Wharfe, mainly.

Yorkshire Fludding: A consequence of rain.

Yorkshire Sudding: What Yorkies do in the bath.

Yorkshire Crudding: The stuff that sticks to your boots after a long stroll in the Dales.

Yorkshire Fudding: Something your Fud does. Obviously.

Yorkshire Nudding: The throwing off of your clothes in Harrogate.

9

Uncle Norman reincarnated as a Yorkshire Pudding

Uncle Norman was, let's say, eccentric. He always said he wanted to be reincarnated as a Yorkshire Pudding because he loved them so much. When he died, Auntie Mabel arranged for us to have Yorkshire Puddings at the funeral tea instead of the usual ham sandwiches. Mrs Dobson from next door was pouring gravy on her Yorkshire puddings when suddenly she screamed: the gravy had formed an N on the pudding. N for Norman…

11

Believe it or not!

In the cement strike of 1926, Brian Howarth of Methley used Yorkshire Pudding batter as mortar when he was building his house, and … it's still standing today!

A Yorkshire GP, Dr Stephen Potente, prescribed Yorkshire Pudding Mixing as physiotherapy for his elderly patients, and … last year one of them ran the Settle Marathon!

Lionel Thorne, for a bet of £3 10s 6d, only uttered the words 'Yorkshire Pudding' for twenty years from 1940 to 1960, and … his first words when he stopped, having won the bet, were "By, I fancy a Yorkshire Pudding"!

Hull man saved by Yorkshire Pudding

Trevor Thornton of Hessle Road yesterday said that he owed his life to the Yorkshire pudding he was carrying to his mother's house last Sunday.

"My mother lives three streets away and we always cook a couple of spare Yorkshire Puddings on a Sunday and take them down to her to have with her dinner. We've asked her to come to our house but she's too independent and I don't mind taking them down.

"The other day the sky was really heavy and it looked like it was going to chuck it down so I set off with the puddings before the rain started.

There was thunder in the air and I could see lightning in the distance and then suddenly there was a huge clap of thunder and lightning struck a tree in Mrs Southern's garden; then lightning set fire to a bush in old Joe Draper's place and I could sense that the storm was getting closer. I instinctively put the Yorkshire Puddings over my head and it's lucky I did because a second later there was a huge flash and lightning struck the puddings, turning them to cinders.

"So the puddings saved my life and all that happened was I got gravy down my face."

Hull Gazette, 4th August 1952

Letters to the Ed

Dear Sir,
Your readers might be amused to hear that, when my grandson asked me about all the planets in the Solar System the other day, and what their relationship was to the Sun, I demonstrated on our kitchen floor using Yorkshire Puddings of different sizes.

I made a small one for Mercury, a larger one for Mars and so on. Uranus took four bowls of mix and Saturn looked very nice with onion rings. Pluto was a tiny pudding at the edge of the kitchen which my husband stood on when he came home from work. This amused us.

Extract from H G Wells's abandoned novel
The Yorkshire Pudding Time Machine

…the time was nigh; the kitchen was filling with the heat of the oven and I could see the pudding rising through the glass. I had on my asbestos suit to prevent charring of my fundament but I was so excited that it felt as if my soul was afire! I glanced at the clock on the wall. Now. Now. I had to do it now. I donned my oven gloves, a present from Polperro. I pulled the huge Yorkshire Pudding from the inferno. I sat it on its plate and, hesitantly, I climbed into the Pudding as though I was climbing into a small canoe. Now. Now. I picked up the Gravy of Time, made from the secret elixir of Frzzskrm and Component X, and poured it over my head. It felt warm. It felt strange. It felt … good. But was anything happening? Was I, in fact, moving backwards through time? Was my Yorkshire Pudding rendering the veil of the unknown dimension to project me back to last week or even further, to the week before last?

Sadly not. The gravy cooled and I sat there looking foolish. More Component X next time.

'The Yorkshire Pudding Song', from the lost Gershwin musical *Almost Midnight in Wakefield*

If you see something risin'
Above the horizon
Then it's really surprisin'
It's a pudding my dear
From Yorkshire...

If you see something groovy
In the morning hazy
And it's covered in gravy
It's a pudding my dear
From Yorkshire...

It's as round as the moon in the sky
And as bright as the look in your eye
And when you feed me I wonder why
I feel like I've wings and I want to fly
And it's because the pudding makes me feel high
Yes the pudding makes me feel high...

If you taste something classy
That puts pounds on your chassis
You grand Yorkshire lassy
It's a pudding my dear
From Yorkshire...

The Yorkshire entry for the 1964 Eurovision Song Contest

When the Eurovision Song Contest was briefly allowed to include entries from regions as well as sovereign states, the Yorkshire entry 'Pudding Pud Pudding Pud' achieved notoriety by amassing less than one vote, a feat hitherto deemed impossible until an unnamed region (Lancashire) refused to vote for any other song unless they were allowed to give a minus vote to the Yorkshire one. The Lancashire voting panel said the song was unbelievably bad; I'm not sure it was so awful compared to a lot of other Eurovision ditties. The lyrics are reproduced opposite — you decide.

Pudding Pud Pudding Pud
Egg, flour, milk
Beat it till it's smooth as silk
Pudding Pud Pudding Pud
Oven nice and hot
If you don't want them I'll eat the lot!
Pudding Pud Pudding Pud

Better than cake and better than flan
Good for a woman and good for a man
Is the Pudding Pud Pudding Pud
Pudding Pud Pudding Pud
(Repeat to fade)

(Maybe you have to have the tune, too…)

Playground skipping rhyme

Grab the spoon
Mix the batter
Make it fly
Make it splatter
If in batter
You will drown
You've got to take
Your britches down!

*collected by folklorist George Norton
in Dalebeck Primary School in 1932*

TOP TIPS

If you find that your sink is impossible
to keep clean, I've found that a quick
scour round with a Yorkshire Pudding
will do the trick.

The pudding can also be utilised for
the cleaning of windows and spectacles,
though obviously not for trousers or hats.

from the *Yorkshirewoman's Magazine*, April 1974

Believe it or not!

Yorkshire Puddings were used in seventeen different ways in an avant-garde production of *South Pacific* by the Skipton WI drama group, and ... the eighteenth way was banned by the police after consultation!

During the severe winter of 1947 a family from Dent kept themselves alive by sleeping in a giant Yorkshire Pudding Igloo for three weeks, and ... when the snow finally melted they carried on living there for eight months!

Cecilia Browton of the Hall, Browton, had a dream before the Derby of 1963 that a horse called Yorkshire Pudding would win, but there were no horses of that name in the race. However, she firmly believed that a horse called Yorkshire Pudding would be entered at the last minute and placed a bet consisting of the entire estate on the horse, and ... it never ran and she died in poverty!

The Yorkshire Pudding Nativity
by Mrs Johnson of Ilkley

My mother always used to tell the story of the Yorkshire Pudding Nativity play they had every year at their school in the Dales.

This would be in the 1920s, and on the appointed day the cook would be in early, making gallons and gallons of batter. Then the school oven had to be really hot and the making of the puddings would begin!

The stable would be made out of Yorkshire Puddings, and Mary and Joseph would arrive at the Inn on a pudding rather than a donkey. When Jesus was born they'd lie him in a soft pudding and a great shining Yorkshire Pudding would appear in the sky. The shepherds would be tending sheep-shaped puddings and the Three Wise Men would bring gifts of pudding, pudding, and pudding.

Then the whole village would sit and eat the puddings!

Merry Christmas!

Fifth annual meeting of the Yorkshire Pudding Ancient History Society

0900: Registration. Tea and coffee served in puddings.

0930: Welcome address by Professor Milton Seed: 'The Yorkshire Pudding as Cultural 'Everyobject'.'

10.15: Professor Doris Clayton: 'Cro-Magnon Woman's Use of the Yorkshire Pudding as Fertility Aid' (with slides).

11.00: Coffee served in puddings.

11.30: Discussion: 'Did the Yorkshire Pudding exist before the Big Bang?'

12.30: Questions. Keep these short enough to be written on the back of a Type C Yorkshire Pudding.

13.00: Lunch. Yorkshire Puddings.

14.00: Professor Alphonse d'Anguishe: 'Was the Ark in fact a Giant Yorkshire Pudding?' 3D models will be on display in the foyer.

14.45: Professor Mahmood Singh: 'Evidence of Yorkshire Puddings Used as Counting Aids by the Mxytcethanian People of prehistoric Peru.'

15.30: Tea. Served in puddings.

15.45: Musical item featuring the London Restored Pudding Orchestra playing sacred dance tunes that were performed on Yorkshire Puddings at the time of King Ethelbert the Damp.

16.30: Depart. Flour Committee to stay behind.

The secret diary of Stephen Mossman, aged 12

Got home from school. Got ready for Alison's fancy dress party. I fancy Alison and I think she fancies me unless anybody is reading this diary in which case go away. I decided a few weeks ago to go to the party as a Yorkshire pudding because I heard Alison say to her best mate Dawn (YUK YUK) that she liked YPs. I'd got my mam to make me a YP costume out of some old curtains and I must say when I looked in the mirror I thought I was in fact looking at a Yorkshire pudding. Daft big brother Jason tried to put me off by saying I looked like a fat kid in a pair of old curtains so when I'm the King of the world he'll die slowly. Got to the fancy Dress party. Alison looked fantastic as Kylie. Good job my Yorkshire pudding costume was long and loose. I walked towards her and she looked at me. "what are you meant to be?" she asked. "Can't you tell? I'm a Yorkshire Pudding!" I said slightly too loudly and then Dawn (YUK YUK) came over with a big jug of orange juice and said "well here's your gravy!" and poured it over my head. Alison laughed and I started crying and ran home. I think she laughed in a sympathetic way, though. I'll get Dawn (YUK YUK) back though. Don't you worry.

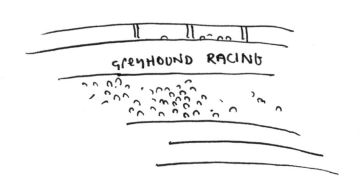

44

Sir,
I find that a Yorkshire Pudding, fresh from the
oven, when placed in bed half an hour before
you retire, will render the bed nice and warm.
NB: Gravy is not advised. Ask my cousin Terence.

Believe it or not!

The biggest ever Yorkshire Pudding was made in Elland in 1961 and measured seventeen miles in circumference! It could be seen from space by Yuri Gagarin!

Attempts by the Yorkshire Pudding Marketing Board to get James Bond to have a Yorkshire Pudding rather than a martini in the film *Dr No* were only turned down when it was revealed that Sean Connery preferred haggis!

If the inventor of the Yorkshire Pudding, Orwell Snaith, had been born in Staffordshire, the Yorkshire Pudding would have had a different name!

47

Mrſ Milton'ſ Handy Pudding Rhyme (1687)

A pudding iſ a marvellouſ thing:
A ſmall one can be a wedding ring!

A Yorkſhire pudding can be uſed
Aſ a poultice if your ſkin iſ bruiſed!

A Yorkſhire pudding forged in fire
Can be uſed on your cart aſ a ſpare tyre!

Take it from me, wife Mrſ Milton
You can uſe a Yorkſhire Pudding to cover your ſtilton!

With a monocle lenſ, ſome gumption and a rope
A Yorkſhire Pudding can become a teleſcope!

If your children are not very clever
Uſe a Yorkſhire Pudding to teach 'em about the weather!*

* EG:
a pudding flung into the ſky
Can repreſent the ſunſhine and iſ pleaſing to the eye!

A pudding placed upon the face
Can repreſent a foggy place!

Yorkshire pudericks

An ingenious glazier called Dave
Had an idea as he showered and shaved
Instead of putty
Use pud batter: that's nutty
But think of the money he saved!

A thing to do with your Yorkshire pud
Is light your fire with it instead of wood.
It crackles and glows
And the smell hits your nose:
Burned Yorkshire — so tasty, so good!

Wise old sayings related to Yorkshire Puddings (some unfathomable)

A Pudding on the plate is worth three in the tin

He's as much use as a wooden Yorkshire Pudding

Too many Puddings lead to padding

The bigger the arm the better the mix

Never leave a Pudding unfinished
if you want to keep your hair

If Puddings were money we'd all ride on dolphins

The quicker the mixing the lighter the Pudding

I'd rather have a Pudding than a disease

54

The short-lived Yorkshire Pudding film industry

Herbert Croall of Tadcaster was fascinated by film and the possibilities of the new popular medium; in the early 1920s, just before the advent of talkies, he produced a number of short films with Yorkshire Puddings at their heart in an attempt to capture a mass market with a love of moving pictures and Yorkshire Puddings.

He was hoping to make a fortune from his films but, after a short period of fame in the village halls and burgeoning cinemas of West Yorkshire, his popularity declined and he became a flour-sculptor in Leeds. Some say that this was because his films all had the same plot but I couldn't possibly comment.

His four surviving short films can be viewed at the Yorkshire Pudding Film Archive:

Molly Wins the Day: in this film, our heroine Molly Methley rescues a drowning cat from the River Aire by sailing into the raging current using her giant Yorkshire Pudding. The cat's owner, Miss M'oney, rewards her with £1 million.

Molly Saves the Day: In this film, our heroine Molly Mirfield rescues a drowning dog from the River Calder by sailing into the raging current using her giant Yorkshire Pudding. The dog's owner, Dave Cash-in-Hand, rewards her with two million pounds.

Molly Rescues the Owl: In this film our heroine Molly Mexborough recues a distressed owl from a greenhouse fire by running into the burning greenhouse using her giant Yorkshire Pudding as protection from the flames. The owl's owner, Lord Chek-Booke, rewards her with £3 million.

Molly Fights the Octopus: In this film our heroine Molly Malton fights a huge octopus that is threatening to attack the village of Slaithwaite, using her giant Yorkshire Pudding as a club. The village squire, Squire Rich-Toff, rewards her with £4 million.

Letters to the editor

Sir,

Does anybody in the Dales remember the practice of using Yorkshire Puddings as scarecrows?

Between the wars when straw was scarce and old jackets and hats were hard to come by, a number of farmers in Arkengarthdale used to tie a Yorkshire Pudding to a post to ward off birds.

The success of this method is not known, but the little-known Yorkshire Dialect poet Seth Teth refers to it in his epic 'Can tha Mix Me Sum Batter Mother, The Crows is a-Gettin on Me Nerves.'

Haiku on the theme of Yorkshire Pudding

In 1876, the distinguished Japanese poet Han Un
visited Halifax as a guest of the Calder Valley
Sino-British Understanding Society. At a banquet
on the Saturday night he partook in a traditional
Yorkshire dinner which, of course, included Yorkshire
puddings. He was so delighted by them that he
wrote three haiku which are reprinted opposite.

O Yorkshire Pudding
You shine like the wide full moon
On the sky's blue plate

From the soft batter
To the hard crunching pudding
Is a life's journey

You call it gravy
I call it Love's Elixir
Soaking my pudding

Believe it or not!

Yorkshire Pudding-flavoured marmalade was taken off the shelves in 1972 after widespread confusion was reported amongst the middle-aged!

Yorkshire Pudding is the 1,354th most popular last meal requested by American prisoners on the night before their execution!

If the inventor of the Yorkshire Pudding, Orwell Snaith, had been born in Leicestershire, the pudding would have had a different name!

A man called John Tabernackle once dreamed that horse called Yorkshire Pudding would win the Grand National and has placed an open £10,000 bet with bookmakers in case a horse called Yorkshire Pudding ever runs in the race!

65

From the programme of the Halifax Symphony Orchestra, autumn 1934

After the interval, the orchestra will present the world premiere of Dr Walter Slattersby's Pudding Concerto, a piece entirely performed on Yorkshire Puddings. Puddings will be hit and struck with various mallets; puddings will have mouthpieces fitted and will be blown like brass instruments; and the Pudding Cello, invented by Dr Slattersby, will be played by the Doctor himself. As he says:

"I had difficulty making the batter thin enough to create pudding-strings that would stretch, but the problem was solved by the application of a little bicarbonate of soda and lard in equal quantities."

Friends of the orchestra will remember Dr Slattersby's controversial Duet for Curd Tart and Racing-Pigeon-Beak Marimba which we premiered last year; his latest effort will be less contentious, we think.

THE YORKSHIRE PUDDING
CUP WINNERS 2011

The *Daily Pudding*

Older readers may recall the short-lived *Daily Pudding*, a newspaper begun in 1937 by Yorkshire Pudding enthusiast Bob 'Puds' Keeling.

Bob's dream was to have a daily source of news and features devoted to his beloved Yorkshire Pudding, and he sunk his entire life savings into what was at best a risky undertaking and at worst a potentially bankrupting total disaster.

The first issue's headline was 'Woman Makes More Yorkshire Puddings Than She Needs' and the recipe was 'Yorkshire Puddings with Added Cauliflower'. The sports pages concentrated on the half-time Yorkshire Puddings that allegedly kept Kettlewell Town on a winning run, and the crossword was a simple grid with all the answers being the words 'Yorkshire' and 'Pudding', though not necessarily in that order.

After three issues the newspaper folded but copies have been known to fetch up to £30,000 on eBay. Search your attics!

Old Yorkshire Pudding weather sayings

When your puds refuse to rise
Then the frost will freeze your thighs
Huddersfield area, 1700s

If your pudding tastes of omelette
Then it will rain and you'll get wet
Skipton, first recorded in 1645

If your pudding gives you the runs
Tomorrow will bring out the Sun
Pickering area, 1876

If you drop your mixture on the floor
Snow will come knocking at your door.
Wakefield, medieval times

From the script of the lost Yorkshire film classic
Frankenstein of the Puddings

FX: A STORM IS RAGING. DR FRANKENSTEIN IS MIXING BATTER IN HIS LABORATORY. HE CRACKS ANOTHER EGG INTO THE BOWL.

Dr Frankenstein: Listen to t' thunder, like sacks o' coil being tipped into t' coil oil! Soon t' leetnin'll be here, and then…

WE SEE A FIGURE ON A SLAB, COVERED IN A BLANKET.

Dr Frankenstein: …and then tha'll come to life, my beauty! All them puddins I mixed! All them puddins I pinched from t' kitchens o' fancy bars and pubs! All them leftover puddins I snatched from rubbish bins at t' back o' hotels and that! And I stitched 'em together into a bloke! A bloke made out of puddins! A pudding bloke! All I need is this…

WE SEE A HUGE VAT OF GRAVY.

Dr Frankenstein:…and this!

HE POINTS TO THE STORM. LIGHTNING IS BEGINNING TO FLASH.

Dr Frankenstein: Tha sees, t' leetnin'll strike them theer electrodes and it'll run like dahn t' wores and then I'll chuck gravy on t' pudding bloke and he'll live! He'll live! Time ter mek moor mixcher! Moor mixcher!!

Yorky the Pudding

Not many people remember this series of children's books from the 1950s, written by the Rev B D Polworth, vicar of St Stan's Church, Idle. Rev Polworth published them himself at the rate of one a year; they proved incredibly popular in the Idle area until the last one was published in 1963. The titles are:

> *Yorky the Pudding*
> *Yorky the Pudding rides in his Gravy Boat*
> *Yorky the Pudding and the Batter Monster*
> *Watch Out Yorky: they're going to eat you!*
> *Yorky and the Hot Oven*
> *Yorky's Great Lard Hunt*
> *Yorky vs Pancake Pete*

If you find any of these books, contact the archivist at the *Dalesman*; they are incredibly and valuable, particularly *Yorky's Great Lard Hunt*, which was actually printed in gravy on Yorkshire Puddings.

Actual names of people who have changed their names to Yorkshire Pudding by deed poll since 1896

Mr Yorkshire Pudding

Mrs Yorkshire Pudding

Yorky Pudding

Yorkshire O'Pudding

York Pud esq

York Shirepudding

Y Orkshirepudding

Msr Yorkshire de Puddinge

YP

YP II

Y Pudd

Y. Pudding

Y-P

Yorkshire McPudding

Yorkevitch Puddingski

Grandma Gawber's pudding days of the week

A reader writes:

My grandma Nellie Gawber was such a fan of the Yorkshire Pudding that she named the days of the week after the humble snack; her way of describing the days is still used by my family.

Sunday:	Pudding Day
Monday:	Cold Pudding Day
Tuesday:	Left-Over Pudding Day
Wednesday:	Oh, Flipping Heck, Let's Just Have a Pudding Day
Thursday:	Is it Pudding Day Yet?
Friday:	Mix the Puddings Day
Saturday:	Let the Pudding Mixture Stand Day

Yorkshire Pudding calendar

January: Frost as white as Yorkshire Pudding batter.

February: Ice cracks like the eggs I use for Yorkshires.

March: Mornings crisp as good Yorkshire Pudding.

April: The garden grows, rising like my puddings in the oven.

May: Sprinkles of tree blossom like sprinkles of flour.

June: Early mornings warm, like the oven door opening.

July: Round pudding sun in the blue sky.

August: Hotter than the lard in my pudding tin.

September: Wheels on the school bus turn like a dropped pudding.

October: Round pudding moon in the night sky.

November: Nights darker than burnt Yorkshire Pudding.

December: Snowman with a pudding face.

Ideas sent to the Patent Office between 1927 and 1977

The Yorkshire Pudding Jigsaw: make, cook, eat.

Yorkshire Pudding Bagpipes: for the Scotsman in exile in Yorkshire.

Yorkshire Pudding Burglar Alarm (plans not submitted)

Yorkshire Pudding Batter-driven Motorbike.

Yorkshire Pudding in tablet form for astronauts.

Yorkshire Pudding Owl-Scarer (plans not submitted).

Yorkshire Pudding Novelty Edible Shower Soap.

Yorkshire Pudding Furniture: simply cook and sit.

Yorkshire Pudding Philosophy Kit (plans not submitted).

Yorkshire Pudding Christmas Decorations: hang and eat.

Yorkshire Pudding Pillow: don't cook 'em for too long.

Yorkshire Pudding Garden Pond (plans not submitted).

Pudding Heck!

Herbert Matlock was a nineteenth-century mill-owner in Holmfirth who was also a staunch Primitive Methodist. He objected to his workers drinking and carousing but most of all he objected to them swearing. He tried a number of methods to get them to clean their language up, from on-the-spot fines to a voluntary swear box and prizes for the workers who swore the least.

In the end, though, he came up with a solution that is still in use around parts of Holmfirth today. He instituted the idea of using the words 'Yorkshire Pudding' instead of the offending language, and it proved a runaway success. Now, instead of blasphemies and profanities, the workers would say 'Pudding Heck!' or 'Yorkshire Pud!' if they dropped a hammer on their toes or if their machine broke down.

Oddly, output increased, but nobody is sure why.

My Mam's Yorkshire Puddings
by Lee Shackleton
aged 7

They taste nicer
Than rice
And they're a different colour
And shape
To grapes
And you put gravy on them
Not like bananas
My dad says they put hairs on your chest
So my Auntie Mabel must have eaten a lot
Because I accidentally saw her getting changed
In the baths
And she must have had a lot of yorkshire puddings
A very lot of yorkshire puddings.

8/10
Very good work Lee. A vivid imagination!
Wait till I see your Auntie Mabel!

Variations on a theme of Yorkshire Puddings, part two

Yorkshire Oudding: The playing of the Yorkshire version of the traditional Middle-eastern instrument, the Oud.

Yorkshire Gudding: The first phrase a Yorkshire ventriloquist has to learn to say.

Yorkshire Wudding: collecting kindling for the fire in Hebden Bridge.

Yorkshire Udding: The milking of a Yorkshire cow.

Yorkshire Dding: The playing of two Yorkshire bells.

Yorkshire Ding: The playing of one Yorkshire bell.

Yorkshire Ing: A damp area of ground favoured by birds.

Yorkshire Ng: That's your opinion.

Yorkshire G: That's my opinion.

Yorkshire double puderick

Bad Billy Bibb was convicted
Of fraud then he was evicted
So his family of five
Keep themselves alive
In a Yorkshire Pudding; it's somewhat restricted

But it's somewhere to sleep and to eat;
Though a pudding's a scratchy old sheet
And the pillow's so hard
It's just like frozen lard
But it's better than life on the street!

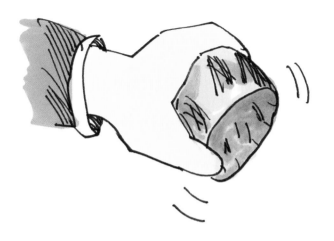

Pudding is first football mascot

Sheffield FC, formed in 1857, have taken the unusual step of employing Colin Treeton to be their match-day 'mascot'.

The idea is that Mr. Treeton will, in the words of the club, "dress as a Yorkshire Pudding to amuse the young folks in the crowd before the game".

from the *Sheffield Telegraph,* 3rd March 1889.

Pudding banned from football club

Sheffield FC, formed in 1857, have taken the unusual step of banning Mr. Colin Treeton from their ground. A club spokesman said that Mr. Treeton, in his role as Yorkshire Pudding-costumed mascot, was meant to amuse the young folks in the crowd before the game and not, in the words of the police report, "incite violence and mayhem by rolling around in the opposition goalmouth during the game, putting off the players by hiding the match ball inside the Yorkshire Pudding costume." Mr. Treeton's trial begins on Tuesday.

from the *Sheffield Telegraph*, 6th March 1889.

Curious duck incident on the River Wharfe, sent in by one of our readers Mrs E H

"The other Saturday I was feeding the swans on the Wharfe with one of my grand-daughters. We normally take bread but this time I'd taken some of my Yorkshire Puddings because I'd cooked them for slightly too long and they were hard and burnt. I didn't know if the ducks would like them but I thought I may as well see. I took one of the puddings and flung it into the river. To my amazement one of the ducks caught it in her bill and threw it to another duck, who proceeded to Frisbee it to yet another duck. I was amazed and my grand-daughter made a film of it on her mobile phone."

Do any other readers have any amusing duck/Yorkshire Pudding/Frisbee anecdotes?

NEW!
'PUDDING FOR MEN'

Men! Are you tired of that 'just-washed' aroma? Are you bored of the same old fragrances? Why not try new Pudding For Men? There's a range of Anti-Perspirant, Deodorant, After-Shave Gravy, Shower Gel and Shampoo with the lingering scent of a Yorkshire Pudding Fresh from the Oven.

Lads ... a couple of dabs of this just before a night out and you'll be guaranteed a night hotter than that oven your mam used to do her Yorkshires in!

Pudding punctuation

The eccentric grammarian Linda Trustworthy was fond of creating new punctuation marks; who can forget her sideways colon(..) which denoted 'a pause of more than five seconds' or her double comma (,,) which meant 'speaker pauses for effect on a Tuesday'.

Perhaps her most notorious mark, however, is the Yorkshire Punc-ding, an outsize circle the size of a small Yorkshire Pudding which she says "denotes exaggeration in a statement of the kind a Yorkshireman might make". She gives the following examples in fake Yorkshire dialect:

By, Ah reckon Yorkshire's t' best county in England

She's t' lovelist lass i' Harrogate

Yes, I think we get the drift.

The Island of Pudding

When HMS *GorBlimey* was sunk in a terrible storm off the Pacific island of Oio'oo'oio in the 1840s, there was just one survivor, a man called Will Bertram.

Will staggered naked to the shore of the uninhabited island and lived there alone for the next thirty years until he was rescued by passing sailors from a kipper fleet.

Alone, that is, except for one possession: a Yorkshire Pudding wrapped in waterproof cloth that Will had been about to eat just as the storm struck.

Over the next three decades the pudding became Bertram's companion (he drew a face on it), his clock (he drew a clock face on it), his calendar (he etched the months on it), his barometer (when it felt wet to the touch he knew it had been raining), his parasol (when the sun was hot), his extra hat (when the nights were cold), his signalling device (he waved it at passing ships for year after year) and his unicycle (on days when it seemed there was nothing left to do but unicycle round the island).

When he was finally rescued he insisted that the Yorkshire pudding had its own cabin on the kipper boat, and when he got back to England he married the pudding and they now live very happily in Helmsley.

An unusual thing to do with a Yorkshire Pudding

Mrs Benson's Year Six class made Yorkshire Puddings and then had to write a sentence at home about 'An Unusual Thing to Do with a Yorkshire Pudding.' Here's some of the homework:

I made a tent out of it and slept all night in it in the garden.

I told our Ronnie it was a piece of Moon Rock and he believed me.

I left it on the bus and a policeman brought it home but there were two bites out of it.

I threw it out of my bedroom window and it flew to Pontefract.

I told our Keith it was a potty and he weed in it. Seven times.

I put my hat on it and pretended it was me but it didn't say anything.

I took it next door and told Mrs. French I'd found it on her drive. She kept it and later I heard her eating it.

I lit a bonfire using it as kindling and the bonfire smelled of Sunday.

I told our Nancy it was a hedgehog that had lost its spines and she cried and said 'POOR HEDGY HOG'

I ate it. Was that wrong?

Slack Pudding Money

Slack is a small village near Heptonstall in West Yorkshire, and the eccentric businessman Jed Green nominated himself as the King of Slack one Saturday afternoon in May 1972, "just for something to do" as he told the local radio station. Amongst his other exploits was the creating of a Slack Currency based around the Yorkshire Pudding; he printed several hundred banknotes which could only be used at his ice-cream parlour. The denominations were:

Half a Pudding: illustrated by a hand about to crack an egg into a bowl.

One Pudding: Illustrated by two hands cracking two eggs into a bowl.

Five Puddings: Illustrated by a tray of steaming Yorkshire Puddings being pulled from an oven.

Ten Puddings: Illustrated by a big jug of gravy being poured over a steaming pudding.

One Hundred Puddings: Illustrated by row after row of steaming puddings on a table. One hundred in all.

The first text message

It's not too well known that the first text message ever sent, in 1998, involved a Yorkshire Pudding. It was sent by Simon Basnett to his dad Adrian, who was testing out a prototype phone for him. Simon was a pioneer of the language of text speak, or **txt spk**, and his first message read:

U lk ypud for lnch?

To which his father replied:

Pardon?

To which Simon replied:

U lk ypud n gravy?

To which his father replied:

Pardon?

To which Simon replied:

Lvly grvy n yr ypud

After which his father gave up and walked round to Simon's house.

Cooking a Yorkshire Pudding

Ingredients:
Flour
Eggs
Milk
Pepper

Method:
Put flour in bowl. That's too much. Pour some back in bag. Careful! Clear it up.

Crack eggs into flour. Careful! Clear them up.

Pour milk in bowl. Careful! That's too much. Clear it up.

Beat mixture. Careful! It's going everywhere!

Beat it some more. Vigorously!

Beat it some more. Vigorously! Now you're being silly. Wipe it up.

Pardon? It looks good on the walls? Hey, you're right.

Put some more Yorkshire Pudding batter on the walls.

Say Mmmmm in appreciation.

Cancel the decorator.